Cesar Chavez

written by **Joeming Dunn**
illustrated by **Rod Espinosa**

magic wagon

visit us at
www.abdopublishing.com

Published by Magic Wagon, a division of the ABDO Publishing Group, 8000 West 78th Street, Edina, Minnesota 55439. Copyright © 2009 by Abdo Consulting Group, Inc. International copyrights reserved in all countries. All rights reserved. No part of this book may be reproduced in any form without written permission from the publisher.
Graphic Planet™ is a trademark and logo of Magic Wagon.

Printed in the United States.

Written by Joeming Dunn
Illustrated by Rod Espinosa
Edited by Stephanie Hedlund and Rochelle Baltzer
Interior layout and design by Antarctic Press
Cover art by Rod Espinosa
Cover design by Neil Klinepier

Library of Congress Cataloging-in-Publication Data

Dunn, Joeming W.
  Cesar Chavez / written by Joeming Dunn ; illustrated by Rod Espinosa.
  p. cm. -- (Bio-Graphics)
  Includes index.
  ISBN 978-1-60270-172-4
  1. Chavez, Cesar, 1927-1993--Juvenile literature. 2. United Farm Workers--History--Juvenile literature. 3. Labor leaders--United States--Biography--Juvenile literature. 4. Mexican American migrant agricultural laborers--Biography--Juvenile literature. 5. Migrant agricultural laborers--Labor unions--United States--History--Juvenile literature. I. Espinosa, Rod. II. Title.

HD6509.C48D86 2009
331.88'13092--dc22
[B]

        2007051501

TABLE of CONTENTS

Timeline

1927 - Cesar Chavez was born on March 31, in Yuma, Arizona.

1942 - Chavez quit school to work full-time in the fields.

1946 - Chavez enlisted in the Navy, where he served for two years.

1948 - Chavez married Helen Fabela.

1952 - Chavez joined the Community Service Organization (CSO) in San Jose, California.

1962 - Chavez founded the National Farm Workers Association (NFWA) with labor leader Dolores Huerta.

1966 - The United Farm Workers (UFW) union was formed.

1988 - Chavez held a 36-day "Fast for Life" to call attention to the health hazards farm workers and their children faced. Many other influential people joined him.

1993 - Chavez died on April 23 in San Luis, Arizona.

1994 - On August 8, President Bill Clinton awarded Chavez a posthumous Medal of Freedom.

Cesar Chavez was a farmer, leader, and activist. He was a man who believed in justice and fair treatment. To see how he became the man he was, we must go back to the beginning...

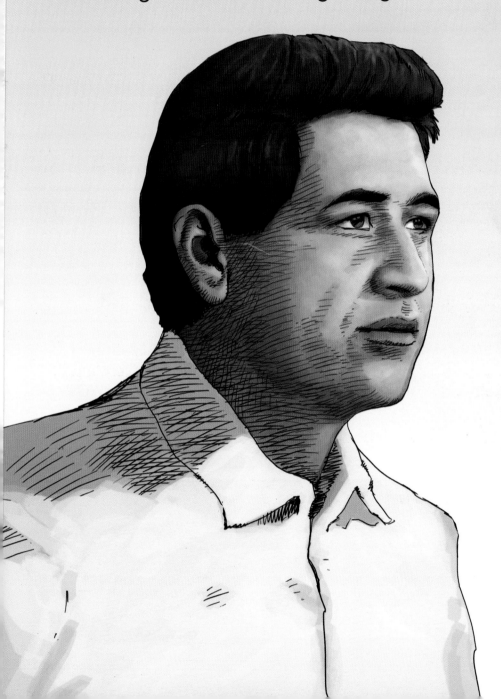

Cesar Chavez was born on March 31, 1927, in Yuma, Arizona. He was born to Librado and Juana Chavez.

WHAT A WONDERFUL BABY.

YOU CAN TELL HE WILL BE A HARD WORKER.

Cesar's family lived in a small adobe house.

He was the second of five children.

Cesar's father was a hardworking man. One day, he was told he would be given 40 acres of land if he cleared 80 acres.

I CAN DO ALL THIS WORK FOR YOU!

IT'S A DEAL. AFTER YOU FINISH YOU GET 40 ACRES.

Librado was cheated in the deal. Once the land was cleared, it was sold to a man named Justus Jackson.

THE LAND IS ALMOST READY. YOU CAN HAVE THE ENTIRE ACREAGE FOR MY PRICE.

JUST LET ME KNOW WHEN IT IS DONE...

Cesar's father talked to a lawyer. The lawyer suggested Librado buy the land.

WHAT SHOULD I DO?

YOU NEED TO GET A LOAN TO BUY THE LAND.

Librado could not pay the interest on the loan. He ended up losing the house and land. His lawyer bought the land from him and sold it back to the original owner!

THIS PROPERTY IS FORECLOSED

Cesar and his family moved back and forth between Arizona and California. In 1939, the Chavezes settled in San Jose, California. They lived in poverty in a barrio called *Sal Si Puedes*, which means "Get Out If You Can."

Welcome
to
California

Arizona

Cesar knew the only way to get out of poverty was to become educated.

Cesar did not like school. It was difficult for him.

Cesar spoke Spanish at home, but he was forbidden to do so at school. Sometimes he was punished for speaking Spanish.

YOU KNOW BETTER THAN TO SPEAK THAT LANGUAGE!

OW! I'M SORRY...

Discrimination was very common in the 1940s. Many places, including schools, were segregated.

WHITES ONLY

I CAN'T EVEN GET A DRINK.

Cesar attended 38 schools before he finished the eighth grade.

After eighth grade, Cesar could not attend school. His father had been injured in an accident, and Cesar had to earn money for the family.

CESAR, YOU NEED TO EARN A LIVING. THE WORK IS TOO HARD FOR YOUR MOTHER.

YES, SIR.

Cesar became a migrant worker to help support his family.

In 1946, Chavez enlisted in the U.S. Navy. He was 17 years old. He served for two years.

I AM PROUD TO SERVE MY COUNTRY.

Cesar married Helen Fabela in 1948. Together they had eight children.

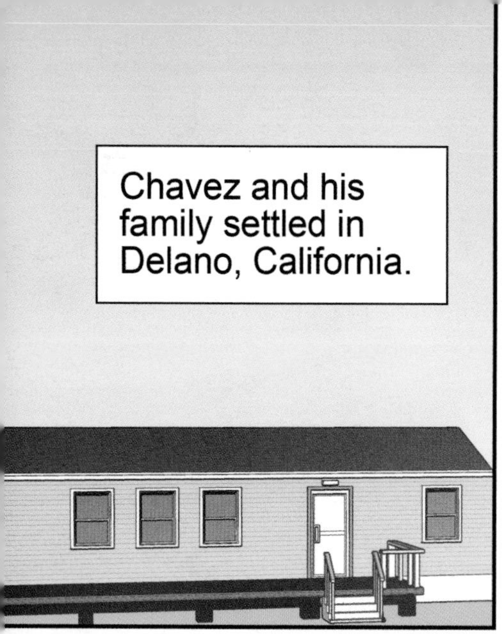
Chavez and his family settled in Delano, California.

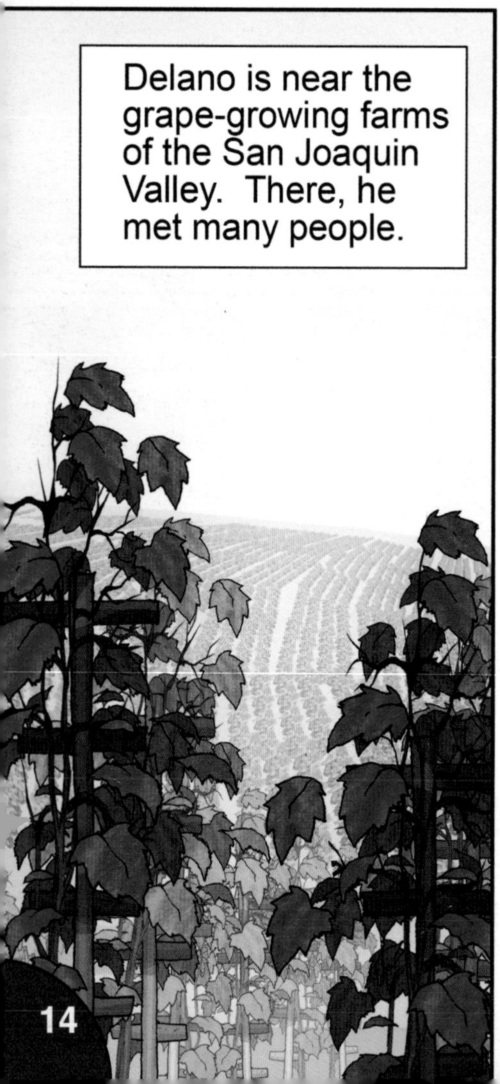
Delano is near the grape-growing farms of the San Joaquin Valley. There, he met many people.

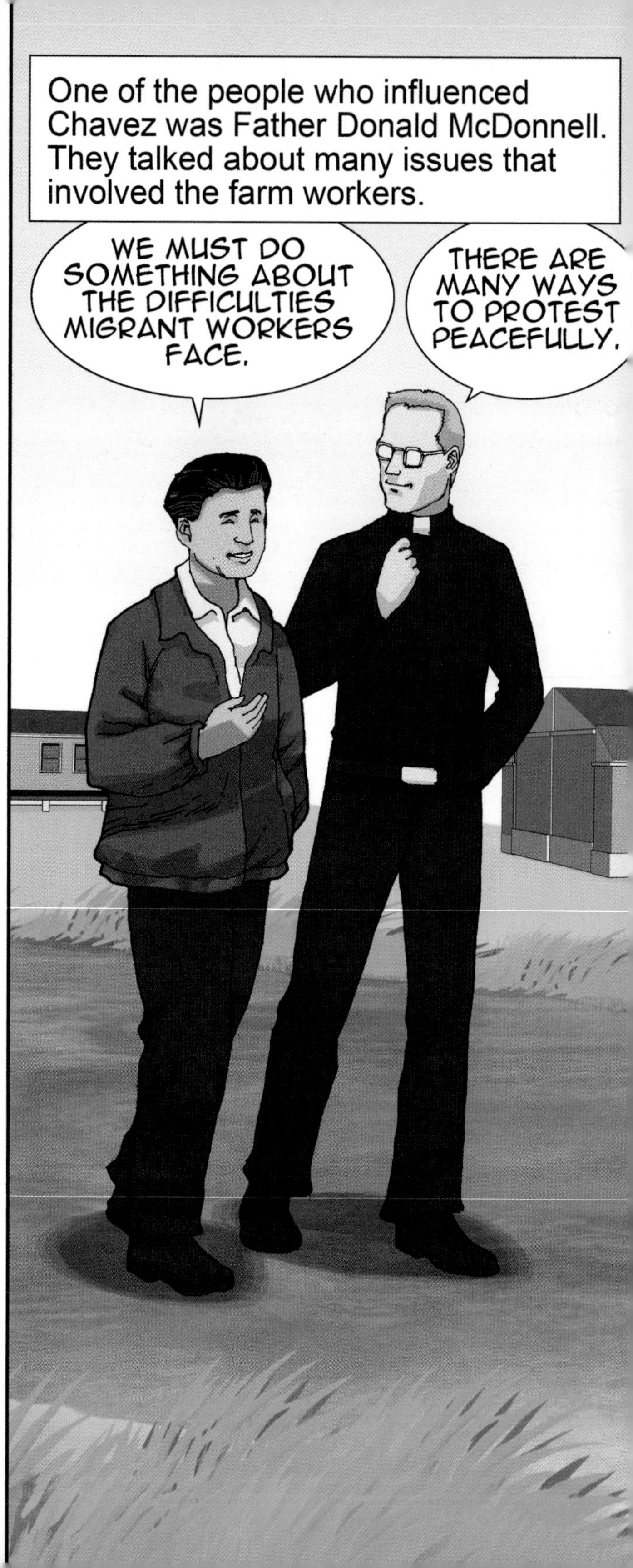
One of the people who influenced Chavez was Father Donald McDonnell. They talked about many issues that involved the farm workers.
WE MUST DO SOMETHING ABOUT THE DIFFICULTIES MIGRANT WORKERS FACE.
THERE ARE MANY WAYS TO PROTEST PEACEFULLY.

Chavez learned about Gandhi and Saint Francis. Both men used forms of nonviolent protest that inspired him.

Chavez also met with a man named Fred Ross. Ross had organized a Latino civil rights group called the Community Services Organization.

TELL ME MORE ABOUT YOUR ORGANIZATION.

WE REPRESENT AND HELP MANY MEXICAN AMERICANS.

Chavez's first job with the organization was to help Latinos register to vote.

WE NEED TO VOTE TO MAKE SURE OUR VOICE IS HEARD.

TELL ME WHAT I NEED TO DO.

Soon Chavez became the national director of the Community Services Organization. He often gave speeches about worker's rights.

Chavez felt more could be done to help farm workers. He met with Dolores Huerta.

WE NEED TO CREATE A UNION FOR THE PEOPLE.

THAT WILL BE DIFFICULT TO DO BUT I'LL HELP YOU.

In 1962, Chavez and Huerta started the National Farm Workers Association. This association would later become the United Farm Workers.

YOU HAVE RIGHTS, AND THIS UNION WILL HELP PROTECT YOUR RIGHTS.

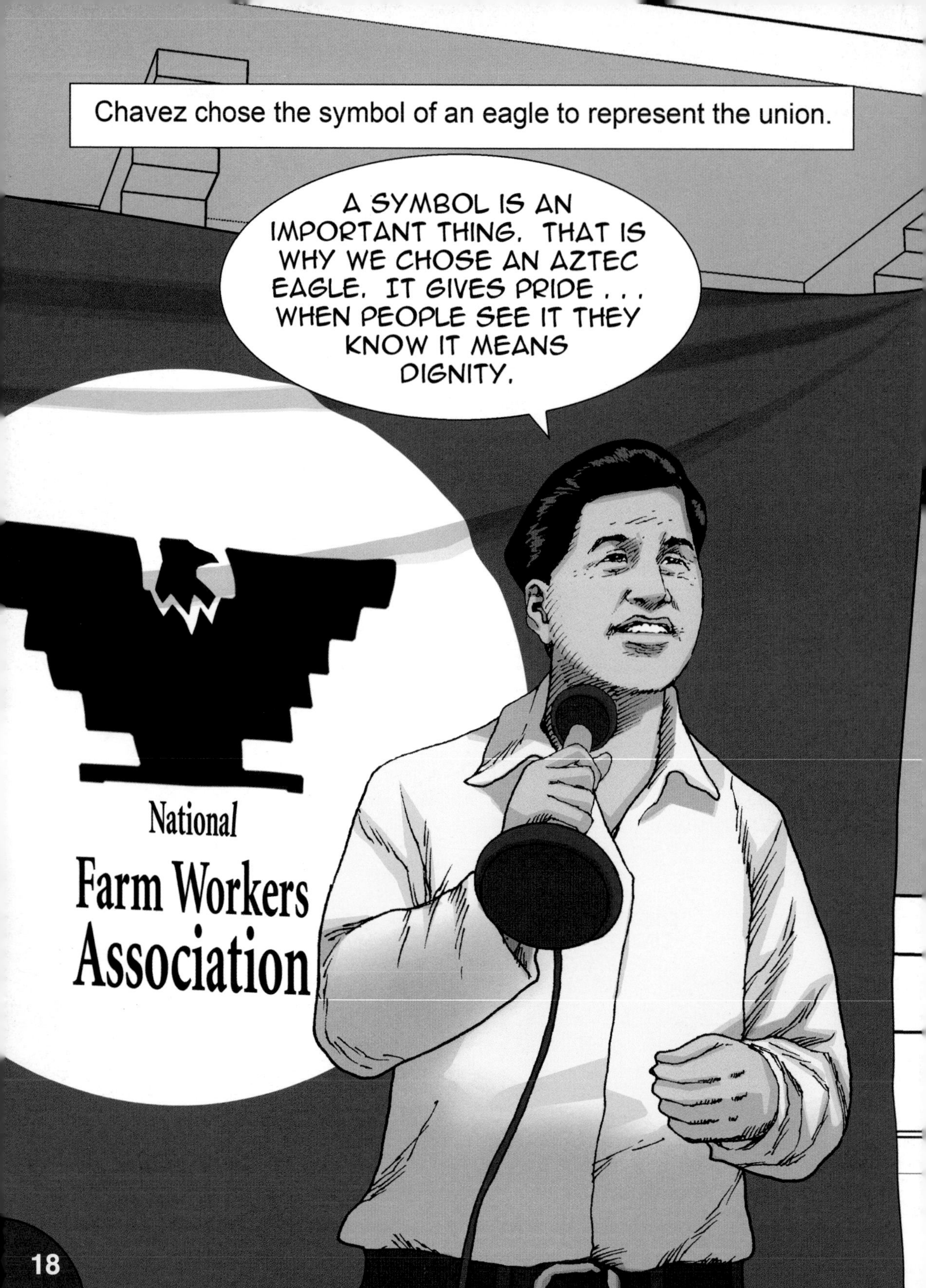
Chavez chose the symbol of an eagle to represent the union.
A SYMBOL IS AN IMPORTANT THING. THAT IS WHY WE CHOSE AN AZTEC EAGLE. IT GIVES PRIDE . . . WHEN PEOPLE SEE IT THEY KNOW IT MEANS DIGNITY.
National Farm Workers Association

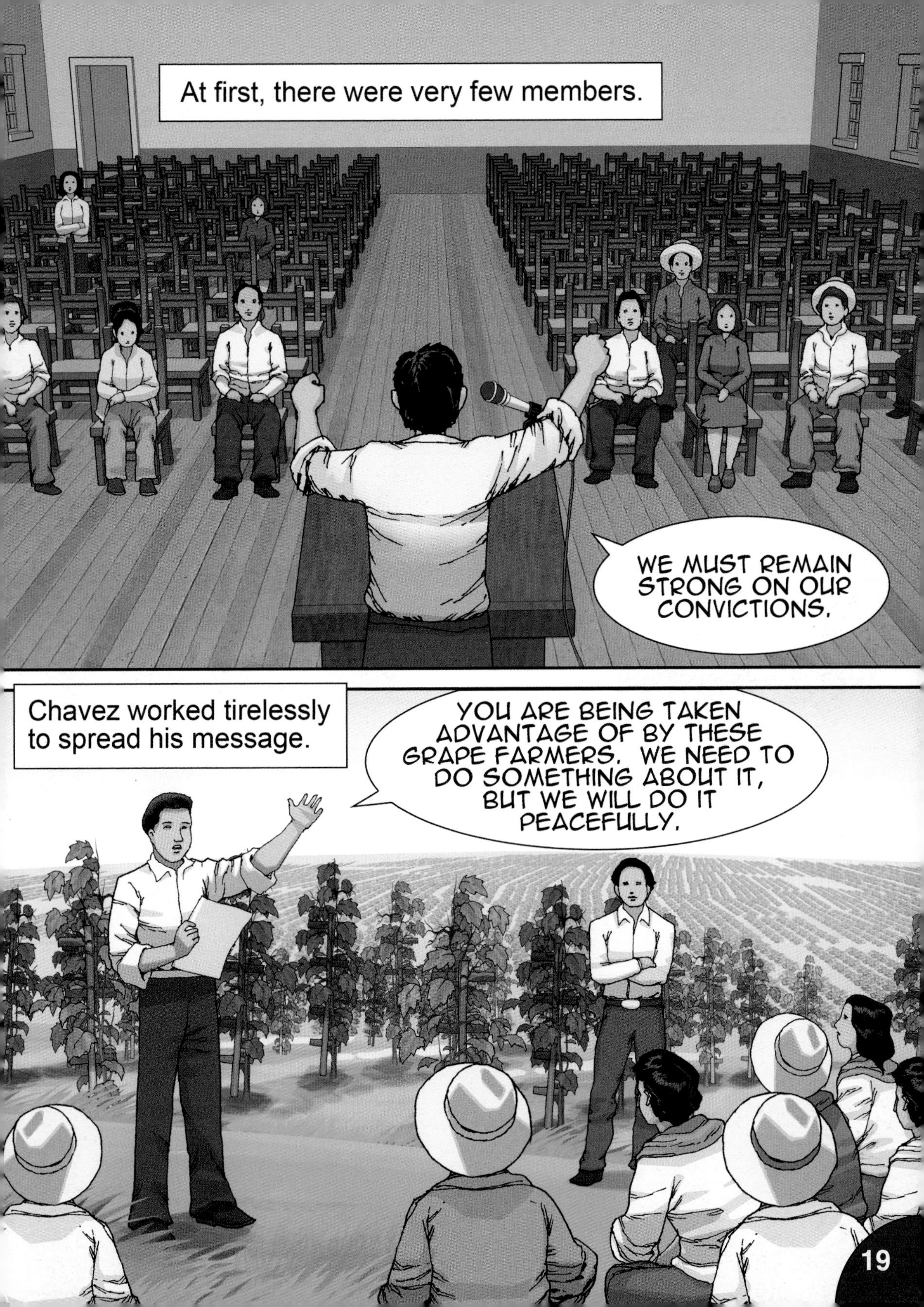

At first, there were very few members.
WE MUST REMAIN STRONG ON OUR CONVICTIONS.
Chavez worked tirelessly to spread his message.
YOU ARE BEING TAKEN ADVANTAGE OF BY THESE GRAPE FARMERS. WE NEED TO DO SOMETHING ABOUT IT, BUT WE WILL DO IT PEACEFULLY.

Chavez was soon joined by another workers union. He organized the Delano grape boycott to protest low wages.

The strikers shouted *huelga*, which means "strike" in Spanish.

He later organized a 340-mile march from Delano to the capitol of Sacramento, California.

Chavez wanted the state to pass laws that would permit farm workers to organize into a union. Having a union would allow for collective bargaining for the workers.

WE ARE ONE VOICE! THEY WILL HAVE TO LISTEN!

The group also encouraged people to boycott grapes as a sign of support.

The UFW took the battle to Washington, D.C.

Many politicians, including Robert Kennedy, supported their cause. This was a major victory for farm workers.

In many areas of the country, people followed Chavez's lead. There were peaceful demonstrations where pickets, boycotts, or strikes were held.

Chavez continued to fight for the protection of both workers and people. Among his concerns was the use of pesticides...

...another was people being denied free and fair elections.

Sometimes, Chavez would fast. This form of protest shed light on the situation. It also showed the sacrifices that came when weak and strong worked together.

I HAVE NOT EATEN IN 36 DAYS, BUT I AM GETTING MY MESSAGE OUT.

During his "Fast for Life" in 1988, many leaders and celebrities joined him. Jesse Jackson, Edward Olmos, Danny Glover, and Whoopi Goldberg showed their support by fasting.

Through Chavez's hard work, the UFW grew to 50,000 members.

He also fought for workers of all types.

Cesar Chavez died on April 23, 1993, in Arizona. At the time, he was working on a trial defending farm workers.

Tens of thousands came to mourn him. It was the largest funeral of any labor leader in the United States.

On August 8, 1994, the Medal of Freedom was given posthumously to Cesar Chavez. It is America's highest civilian honor.

Chavez is celebrated in California every March 31 with a state holiday.

He is remembered with streets, buildings, and stamps with his name and image. He was also nominated for the Nobel Peace Prize three times.

Cesar Chavez had great respect for himself and his community. He showed that with great faith, peace, and hard work, we all can make the world a better place.

Fair Wages

Just Treatment

Workers Rights

Further Reading

Guzmán, Lila, and Guzmán, Rick. *César Chávez: Fighting for Fairness.* New Jersey: Enslow Publishers Inc., 2006.

McLeese, Don. *Cesar E. Chavez.* Florida: Rourke Publishing, LLC, 2002.

Wadsworth, Ginger. *Cesar Chavez.* On My Own Biography. Minneapolis: Lerner Publishing Group, 2005.

Wheeler, Jill C. *Cesar Chavez.* Breaking Barriers. Edina: ABDO Publishing Company, 2003.

National
Farm Workers
Association

Glossary

barrio - a Spanish-speaking neighborhood in the United States.

boycott - to refuse to deal with a person, a store, or an organization until it agrees to certain conditions.

collective bargaining - negotiation between an employer and a labor union usually on wages, hours, and working conditions.

conviction - a strong persuasion or belief.

discrimination - unfair treatment based on factors such as a person's race, religion, or gender.

migrant worker - a person who moves regularly in order to find work, especially in harvesting crops.

posthumous - after a person's death.

segregation - the separation of an individual or a group from a larger group.

Web Sites

To learn more about Cesar Chavez, visit ABDO Publishing Company on the World Wide Web at **www.abdopublishing.com.** Web sites about Chavez are featured on our Book Links page. These links are routinely monitored and updated to provide the most current information available.

Index